Date: _____

Dear Santa,

This year I've been: ☐ mostly good.   ☐ I'd rather not say. I'll try better next year.

I know you'll bring me something great, but here is some info that might be helpful:

My Favorite Color is:

_ _

My Favorite kind of book would be about:

_ _

If I could have any toy for Christmas it would be:

_ _

My favorite kind of candy treat is:

_ _

Thank you, Santa, for your hard work bringing toys to boys and girls all over the world. You are so nice! Please tell Mrs. Claus, the elves, and the reindeer hello from me.

Love,

_ _ _ _ _ _ _ _ _ _ _

Here is a picture of my family. They are my favorite part of Christmas:

Christmas Master Checklist

{in September & October}

- ○ Start adding important dates to your holiday calendar
- ○ Create a budget
- ○ Make Gift Lists
    - ○ Make a list of stocking stuffers
    - ○ Make a shopping list
    - ○ Make homemade gifts list
- ○ _____
- ○ _____
- ○ _____
- ○ _____

{in November}

- ○ Make/buy Christmas cards
- ○ Schedule Christmas photos
- ○ Plan holiday parties
- ○ Start baking items that can be frozen
- ○ Address your Christmas cards
- ○ Put up your Christmas tree and decorations
- ○ Stock up on baking supplies
- ○ Start buying gifts
- ○ Start to declutter and deep clean
- ○ Set up a wrapping station and wrap gifts as you buy them.
- ○ _____
- ○ _____
- ○ _____
- ○ _____

{in December}
- ○ Start your Advent calendar
- ○ Finish baking
- ○ Finish Shopping
- ○ Deliver food gifts
- ○ Mail Christmas Cards
- ○ Plan Holiday meals and create lists
- ○ Shop for Holiday meals
- ○ _____
- ○ _____
- ○ _____

{Christmas Week}
- ○ Finish up last minute shopping
- ○ Charge batteries and clear memory cards
- ○ _____
- ○ _____
- ○ _____
- ○ _____

{After Christmas}
- ○ Write and send your thank you cards
- ○ Make notes about decorations or traditions you want to continue
- ○ Take down decorations
- ○ _____
- ○ _____
- ○ _____
- ○ _____

December

Sunday	Monday	Tuesday	Wednesday	Thursday	Friday	Saturday

NOTES

Dec. 20

-
-
-
-
-
-
-
-
-
-
-
-
-
-

Dec. 21

-
-
-
-
-
-
-
-
-
-
-
-
-
-

Dec. 22

-
-
-
-
-
-
-
-
-
-
-

Dec. 23

-
-
-
-
-
-
-
-
-
-
-

Christmas Eve

-
-
-
-
-
-
-
-
-
-
-
-
-
-
-
-
-
-
-
-
-
-
-

Notes

_____
_____
_____
_____
_____

Christmas Day

-
-
-
-
-
-
-
-
-
-
-
-
-
-
-
-
-
-
-
-
-
-
-

Notes

_____
_____
_____
_____
_____

Christmas Menu Planner

Date: _____   Time: _____

Appetizers

○ _____   ○ _____
○ _____   ○ _____

Main Dishes

○ _____   ○ _____
○ _____   ○ _____
○ _____   ○ _____

Side Dishes

○ _____   ○ _____
○ _____   ○ _____

Desserts

○ _____   ○ _____
○ _____   ○ _____

Notes: _____
_____
_____
_____
_____
_____
_____
_____

Christmas
Shopping List

#

Christmas Menu Planner

Date: _____   Time: _____

Appetizers

○ _____   ○ _____
○ _____   ○ _____

Main Dishes

○ _____   ○ _____
○ _____   ○ _____
○ _____   ○ _____

Side Dishes

○ _____   ○ _____
○ _____   ○ _____

Desserts

○ _____   ○ _____
○ _____   ○ _____

Notes: _____
_____
_____
_____
_____
_____
_____

Christmas
Shopping List

Date: _____ Time: _____

Appetizers

○ _____ ○ _____
○ _____ ○ _____

Main Dishes

○ _____ ○ _____
○ _____ ○ _____
○ _____ ○ _____

Side Dishes

○ _____ ○ _____
○ _____ ○ _____

Desserts

○ _____ ○ _____
○ _____ ○ _____

Notes: _____
_____
_____
_____
_____
_____
_____
_____

Christmas
Shopping List

Christmas Dinner Recipes

Recipe: _____ ○ Prepare ahead of time
Source: _____ Est. cost: $ _____
  Prep time: _____   Cook time: _____   Temp: _____
  Ingredients needed: _____
  _____
  _____
Notes: _____
_____
_____
_____

Recipe: _____ ○ Prepare ahead of time
Source: _____ Est. cost: $ _____
  Prep time: _____   Cook time: _____   Temp: _____
  Ingredients needed: _____
  _____
  _____
Notes: _____
_____
_____
_____

Recipe: _____ ○ Prepare ahead of time
Source: _____ Est. cost: $ _____
  Prep time: _____   Cook time: _____   Temp: _____
  Ingredients needed: _____
  _____
Notes: _____
_____
_____

Christmas Dinner Recipes

Recipe _____ ○ Prepare ahead of time
Source _____ Est. cost: $ _____
　　Prep time: _____ Cook time: _____ Temp: _____
　　Ingredients needed _____
_____
Notes _____
_____
_____

Recipe _____ ○ Prepare ahead of time
Source _____ Est. cost: $ _____
　　Prep time: _____ Cook time: _____ Temp: _____
　　Ingredients needed _____
_____
Notes _____
_____
_____

Recipe _____ ○ Prepare ahead of time
Source _____ Est. cost: $ _____
　　Prep time: _____ Cook time: _____ Temp: _____
　　Ingredients needed _____
_____
Notes _____
_____
_____

Christmas Dinner Recipes

Recipe: _____ ○ Prepare ahead of time
Source: _____ Est. cost: $ _____
    Prep time: _____ Cook time: _____ Temp: _____
    Ingredients needed: _____
_____
_____
Notes: _____
_____
_____

Recipe: _____ ○ Prepare ahead of time
Source: _____ Est. cost: $ _____
    Prep time: _____ Cook time: _____ Temp: _____
    Ingredients needed: _____
_____
_____
Notes: _____
_____
_____

Recipe: _____ ○ Prepare ahead of time
Source: _____ Est. cost: $ _____
    Prep time: _____ Cook time: _____ Temp: _____
    Ingredients needed: _____
_____
_____
Notes: _____
_____
_____

Christmas Dinner Recipes

Recipe: _____ ○ Prepare ahead of time
Source: _____ Est. cost: $ _____
    Prep time: _____ Cook time: _____ Temp: _____
    Ingredients needed: _____
_____
_____
Notes: _____
_____
_____
_____

Recipe: _____ ○ Prepare ahead of time
Source: _____ Est. cost: $ _____
    Prep time: _____ Cook time: _____ Temp: _____
    Ingredients needed: _____
_____
_____
Notes: _____
_____
_____
_____

Recipe: _____ ○ Prepare ahead of time
Source: _____ Est. cost: $ _____
    Prep time: _____ Cook time: _____ Temp: _____
    Ingredients needed: _____
_____
_____
Notes: _____
_____
_____
_____

Christmas Dinner Recipes

Recipe: _____ ○ Prepare ahead of time
Source: _____ Est. cost: $ _____
    Prep time: _____ Cook time: _____ Temp: _____
    Ingredients needed: _____
_____
_____
Notes: _____
_____
_____

Recipe: _____ ○ Prepare ahead of time
Source: _____ Est. cost: $ _____
    Prep time: _____ Cook time: _____ Temp: _____
    Ingredients needed: _____
_____
_____
Notes: _____
_____
_____

Recipe: _____ ○ Prepare ahead of time
Source: _____ Est. cost: $ _____
    Prep time: _____ Cook time: _____ Temp: _____
    Ingredients needed: _____
_____
_____
Notes: _____
_____
_____

Christmas Dinner Recipes

Recipe: _____ ○ Prepare ahead of time
Source: _____ Est. cost: $ _____
   Prep time: _____   Cook time: _____   Temp: _____
   Ingredients needed: _____
_____
Notes: _____
_____
_____

Recipe: _____ ○ Prepare ahead of time
Source: _____ Est. cost: $ _____
   Prep time: _____   Cook time: _____   Temp: _____
   Ingredients needed: _____
_____
Notes: _____
_____
_____

Recipe: _____ ○ Prepare ahead of time
Source: _____ Est. cost: $ _____
   Prep time: _____   Cook time: _____   Temp: _____
   Ingredients needed: _____
_____
Notes: _____
_____
_____

Christmas Card List

Name:	Sent ○	Sent ○	Sent ○	Sent ○
Address:	Rec'd ○	Rec'd ○	Rec'd ○	Rec'd ○
	Notes			
City, State, Zip:				

○ Card ○ Newsletter ○ Card & Newsletter ○ Family Portrait

Name:	Sent ○	Sent ○	Sent ○	Sent ○
Address:	Rec'd ○	Rec'd ○	Rec'd ○	Rec'd ○
	Notes			
City, State, Zip:				

○ Card ○ Newsletter ○ Card & Newsletter ○ Family Portrait

Name:	Sent ○	Sent ○	Sent ○	Sent ○
Address:	Rec'd ○	Rec'd ○	Rec'd ○	Rec'd ○
	Notes			
City, State, Zip:				

○ Card ○ Newsletter ○ Card & Newsletter ○ Family Portrait

Name:	Sent ○	Sent ○	Sent ○	Sent ○
Address:	Rec'd ○	Rec'd ○	Rec'd ○	Rec'd ○
	Notes			
City, State, Zip:				

○ Card ○ Newsletter ○ Card & Newsletter ○ Family Portrait

Name:	Sent ○	Sent ○	Sent ○	Sent ○
Address:	Rec'd ○	Rec'd ○	Rec'd ○	Rec'd ○
	Notes			
City, State, Zip:				

○ Card ○ Newsletter ○ Card & Newsletter ○ Family Portrait

Name:	Sent ○	Sent ○	Sent ○	Sent ○
Address:	Rec'd ○	Rec'd ○	Rec'd ○	Rec'd ○
	Notes			
City, State, Zip:				

○ Card ○ Newsletter ○ Card & Newsletter ○ Family Portrait

BOUGHT/MADE
WRAPPED
GIVEN

NAME	GIFT	BUDGET	✓	✓	✓
			☐	☐	☐
			☐	☐	☐
			☐	☐	☐
			☐	☐	☐
			☐	☐	☐
			☐	☐	☐
			☐	☐	☐
			☐	☐	☐
			☐	☐	☐
			☐	☐	☐
			☐	☐	☐

TOTAL

Christmas Card List

Name:	Sent ○	Sent ○	Sent ○	Sent ○
Address:	Rec'd ○	Rec'd ○	Rec'd ○	Rec'd ○
	Notes:			
City, State, Zip:				
○ Card ○ Newsletter ○ Card & Newsletter	○ Family Portrait			

Name:	Sent ○	Sent ○	Sent ○	Sent ○
Address:	Rec'd ○	Rec'd ○	Rec'd ○	Rec'd ○
	Notes:			
City, State, Zip:				
○ Card ○ Newsletter ○ Card & Newsletter	○ Family Portrait			

Name:	Sent ○	Sent ○	Sent ○	Sent ○
Address:	Rec'd ○	Rec'd ○	Rec'd ○	Rec'd ○
	Notes:			
City, State, Zip:				
○ Card ○ Newsletter ○ Card & Newsletter	○ Family Portrait			

Name:	Sent ○	Sent ○	Sent ○	Sent ○
Address:	Rec'd ○	Rec'd ○	Rec'd ○	Rec'd ○
	Notes:			
City, State, Zip:				
○ Card ○ Newsletter ○ Card & Newsletter	○ Family Portrait			

Name:	Sent ○	Sent ○	Sent ○	Sent ○
Address:	Rec'd ○	Rec'd ○	Rec'd ○	Rec'd ○
	Notes:			
City, State, Zip:				
○ Card ○ Newsletter ○ Card & Newsletter	○ Family Portrait			

Name:	Sent ○	Sent ○	Sent ○	Sent ○
Address:	Rec'd ○	Rec'd ○	Rec'd ○	Rec'd ○
	Notes:			
City, State, Zip:				
○ Card ○ Newsletter ○ Card & Newsletter	○ Family Portrait			

Gift Planner

BOUGHT/MADE
WRAPPED
GIVEN

NAME	GIFT	BUDGET	✓	✓	✓
			☐	☐	☐
			☐	☐	☐
			☐	☐	☐
			☐	☐	☐
			☐	☐	☐
			☐	☐	☐
			☐	☐	☐
			☐	☐	☐
			☐	☐	☐
			☐	☐	☐
			☐	☐	☐

TOTAL

Christmas Card List

Name:	Sent O	Sent O	Sent O	Sent O
Address:	Rec'd O	Rec'd O	Rec'd O	Rec'd O
	Notes:			
City, State, Zip:				
O Card　　O Newsletter　　O Card & Newsletter	O Family Portrait			

Name:	Sent O	Sent O	Sent O	Sent O
Address:	Rec'd O	Rec'd O	Rec'd O	Rec'd O
	Notes:			
City, State, Zip:				
O Card　　O Newsletter　　O Card & Newsletter	O Family Portrait			

Name:	Sent O	Sent O	Sent O	Sent O
Address:	Rec'd O	Rec'd O	Rec'd O	Rec'd O
	Notes:			
City, State, Zip:				
O Card　　O Newsletter　　O Card & Newsletter	O Family Portrait			

Name:	Sent O	Sent O	Sent O	Sent O
Address:	Rec'd O	Rec'd O	Rec'd O	Rec'd O
	Notes:			
City, State, Zip:				
O Card　　O Newsletter　　O Card & Newsletter	O Family Portrait			

Name:	Sent O	Sent O	Sent O	Sent O
Address:	Rec'd O	Rec'd O	Rec'd O	Rec'd O
	Notes:			
City, State, Zip:				
O Card　　O Newsletter　　O Card & Newsletter	O Family Portrait			

Name:	Sent O	Sent O	Sent O	Sent O
Address:	Rec'd O	Rec'd O	Rec'd O	Rec'd O
	Notes:			
City, State, Zip:				
O Card　　O Newsletter　　O Card & Newsletter	O Family Portrait			

BOUGHT/MADE
WRAPPED
GIVEN

NAME	GIFT	BUDGET	✓	✓	✓

TOTAL

Christmas Card List

Name:	Sent ○	Sent ○	Sent ○	Sent ○
Address:	Rec'd ○	Rec'd ○	Rec'd ○	Rec'd ○
	Notes:			
City, State, Zip:				

○ Card ○ Newsletter ○ Card & Newsletter ○ Family Portrait

Name:	Sent ○	Sent ○	Sent ○	Sent ○
Address:	Rec'd ○	Rec'd ○	Rec'd ○	Rec'd ○
	Notes:			
City, State, Zip:				

○ Card ○ Newsletter ○ Card & Newsletter ○ Family Portrait

Name:	Sent ○	Sent ○	Sent ○	Sent ○
Address:	Rec'd ○	Rec'd ○	Rec'd ○	Rec'd ○
	Notes:			
City, State, Zip:				

○ Card ○ Newsletter ○ Card & Newsletter ○ Family Portrait

Name:	Sent ○	Sent ○	Sent ○	Sent ○
Address:	Rec'd ○	Rec'd ○	Rec'd ○	Rec'd ○
	Notes:			
City, State, Zip:				

○ Card ○ Newsletter ○ Card & Newsletter ○ Family Portrait

Name:	Sent ○	Sent ○	Sent ○	Sent ○
Address:	Rec'd ○	Rec'd ○	Rec'd ○	Rec'd ○
	Notes:			
City, State, Zip:				

○ Card ○ Newsletter ○ Card & Newsletter ○ Family Portrait

Name:	Sent ○	Sent ○	Sent ○	Sent ○
Address:	Rec'd ○	Rec'd ○	Rec'd ○	Rec'd ○
	Notes:			
City, State, Zip:				

○ Card ○ Newsletter ○ Card & Newsletter ○ Family Portrait

Gift Planner

BOUGHT/MADE
WRAPPED
GIVEN
✓ ✓ ✓

NAME	GIFT	BUDGET			
			☐	☐	☐
			☐	☐	☐
			☐	☐	☐
			☐	☐	☐
			☐	☐	☐
			☐	☐	☐
			☐	☐	☐
			☐	☐	☐
			☐	☐	☐
			☐	☐	☐

TOTAL

Christmas Card List

Name:	Sent ○	Sent ○	Sent ○	Sent ○
Address:	Rec'd ○	Rec'd ○	Rec'd ○	Rec'd ○
	Notes:			
City, State, Zip:				
○ Card ○ Newsletter ○ Card & Newsletter ○ Family Portrait				

Name:	Sent ○	Sent ○	Sent ○	Sent ○
Address:	Rec'd ○	Rec'd ○	Rec'd ○	Rec'd ○
	Notes:			
City, State, Zip:				
○ Card ○ Newsletter ○ Card & Newsletter ○ Family Portrait				

Name:	Sent ○	Sent ○	Sent ○	Sent ○
Address:	Rec'd ○	Rec'd ○	Rec'd ○	Rec'd ○
	Notes:			
City, State, Zip:				
○ Card ○ Newsletter ○ Card & Newsletter ○ Family Portrait				

Name:	Sent ○	Sent ○	Sent ○	Sent ○
Address:	Rec'd ○	Rec'd ○	Rec'd ○	Rec'd ○
	Notes:			
City, State, Zip:				
○ Card ○ Newsletter ○ Card & Newsletter ○ Family Portrait				

Name:	Sent ○	Sent ○	Sent ○	Sent ○
Address:	Rec'd ○	Rec'd ○	Rec'd ○	Rec'd ○
	Notes:			
City, State, Zip:				
○ Card ○ Newsletter ○ Card & Newsletter ○ Family Portrait				

Name:	Sent ○	Sent ○	Sent ○	Sent ○
Address:	Rec'd ○	Rec'd ○	Rec'd ○	Rec'd ○
	Notes:			
City, State, Zip:				
○ Card ○ Newsletter ○ Card & Newsletter ○ Family Portrait				

Gift Planner

BOUGHT/MADE
WRAPPED
GIVEN

NAME	GIFT	BUDGET	✓	✓	✓
			☐	☐	☐
			☐	☐	☐
			☐	☐	☐
			☐	☐	☐
			☐	☐	☐
			☐	☐	☐
			☐	☐	☐
			☐	☐	☐
			☐	☐	☐
			☐	☐	☐
			☐	☐	☐

TOTAL

Christmas Card List

Name:	Sent ○	Sent ○	Sent ○	Sent ○
Address:	Rec'd ○	Rec'd ○	Rec'd ○	Rec'd ○
	Notes:			
City, State, Zip:				

○ Card ○ Newsletter ○ Card & Newsletter ○ Family Portrait

Name:	Sent ○	Sent ○	Sent ○	Sent ○
Address:	Rec'd ○	Rec'd ○	Rec'd ○	Rec'd ○
	Notes:			
City, State, Zip:				

○ Card ○ Newsletter ○ Card & Newsletter ○ Family Portrait

Name:	Sent ○	Sent ○	Sent ○	Sent ○
Address:	Rec'd ○	Rec'd ○	Rec'd ○	Rec'd ○
	Notes:			
City, State, Zip:				

○ Card ○ Newsletter ○ Card & Newsletter ○ Family Portrait

Name:	Sent ○	Sent ○	Sent ○	Sent ○
Address:	Rec'd ○	Rec'd ○	Rec'd ○	Rec'd ○
	Notes:			
City, State, Zip:				

○ Card ○ Newsletter ○ Card & Newsletter ○ Family Portrait

Name:	Sent ○	Sent ○	Sent ○	Sent ○
Address:	Rec'd ○	Rec'd ○	Rec'd ○	Rec'd ○
	Notes:			
City, State, Zip:				

○ Card ○ Newsletter ○ Card & Newsletter ○ Family Portrait

Name:	Sent ○	Sent ○	Sent ○	Sent ○
Address:	Rec'd ○	Rec'd ○	Rec'd ○	Rec'd ○
	Notes:			
City, State, Zip:				

○ Card ○ Newsletter ○ Card & Newsletter ○ Family Portrait

Gift Planner

NAME	GIFT	BUDGET	BOUGHT/MADE	WRAPPED	GIVEN
			☐	☐	☐
			☐	☐	☐
			☐	☐	☐
			☐	☐	☐
			☐	☐	☐
			☐	☐	☐
			☐	☐	☐
			☐	☐	☐
			☐	☐	☐
			☐	☐	☐

TOTAL

Christmas Card List

	Sent ○	Sent ○	Sent ○	Sent ○
Name:	Rec'd ○	Rec'd ○	Rec'd ○	Rec'd ○
Address:	Notes			
City, State, Zip:				
○ Card ○ Newsletter ○ Card & Newsletter ○ Family Portrait				

	Sent ○	Sent ○	Sent ○	Sent ○
Name:	Rec'd ○	Rec'd ○	Rec'd ○	Rec'd ○
Address:	Notes			
City, State, Zip:				
○ Card ○ Newsletter ○ Card & Newsletter ○ Family Portrait				

	Sent ○	Sent ○	Sent ○	Sent ○
Name:	Rec'd ○	Rec'd ○	Rec'd ○	Rec'd ○
Address:	Notes			
City, State, Zip:				
○ Card ○ Newsletter ○ Card & Newsletter ○ Family Portrait				

	Sent ○	Sent ○	Sent ○	Sent ○
Name:	Rec'd ○	Rec'd ○	Rec'd ○	Rec'd ○
Address:	Notes			
City, State, Zip:				
○ Card ○ Newsletter ○ Card & Newsletter ○ Family Portrait				

	Sent ○	Sent ○	Sent ○	Sent ○
Name:	Rec'd ○	Rec'd ○	Rec'd ○	Rec'd ○
Address:	Notes			
City, State, Zip:				
○ Card ○ Newsletter ○ Card & Newsletter ○ Family Portrait				

	Sent ○	Sent ○	Sent ○	Sent ○
Name:	Rec'd ○	Rec'd ○	Rec'd ○	Rec'd ○
Address:	Notes			
City, State, Zip:				
○ Card ○ Newsletter ○ Card & Newsletter ○ Family Portrait				

BOUGHT/MADE
WRAPPED
GIVEN

NAME	GIFT	BUDGET	✓	✓	✓
			☐	☐	☐
			☐	☐	☐
			☐	☐	☐
			☐	☐	☐
			☐	☐	☐
			☐	☐	☐
			☐	☐	☐
			☐	☐	☐
			☐	☐	☐
			☐	☐	☐

TOTAL

Christmas Card List

Name:	Sent ○	Sent ○	Sent ○	Sent ○
Address:	Rec'd ○	Rec'd ○	Rec'd ○	Rec'd ○
	Notes:			
City, State, Zip:				

○ Card   ○ Newsletter   ○ Card & Newsletter   ○ Family Portrait

Name:	Sent ○	Sent ○	Sent ○	Sent ○
Address:	Rec'd ○	Rec'd ○	Rec'd ○	Rec'd ○
	Notes:			
City, State, Zip:				

○ Card   ○ Newsletter   ○ Card & Newsletter   ○ Family Portrait

Name:	Sent ○	Sent ○	Sent ○	Sent ○
Address:	Rec'd ○	Rec'd ○	Rec'd ○	Rec'd ○
	Notes:			
City, State, Zip:				

○ Card   ○ Newsletter   ○ Card & Newsletter   ○ Family Portrait

Name:	Sent ○	Sent ○	Sent ○	Sent ○
Address:	Rec'd ○	Rec'd ○	Rec'd ○	Rec'd ○
	Notes:			
City, State, Zip:				

○ Card   ○ Newsletter   ○ Card & Newsletter   ○ Family Portrait

Name:	Sent ○	Sent ○	Sent ○	Sent ○
Address:	Rec'd ○	Rec'd ○	Rec'd ○	Rec'd ○
	Notes:			
City, State, Zip:				

○ Card   ○ Newsletter   ○ Card & Newsletter   ○ Family Portrait

Name:	Sent ○	Sent ○	Sent ○	Sent ○
Address:	Rec'd ○	Rec'd ○	Rec'd ○	Rec'd ○
	Notes:			
City, State, Zip:				

○ Card   ○ Newsletter   ○ Card & Newsletter   ○ Family Portrait

Gift Planner

BOUGHT/MADE
WRAPPED
GIVEN

NAME	GIFT	BUDGET	✓	✓	✓

TOTAL

Christmas Card List

Name:	Sent ○	Sent ○	Sent ○	Sent ○
Address:	Rec'd ○	Rec'd ○	Rec'd ○	Rec'd ○
	Notes:			
City, State, Zip:				
○ Card ○ Newsletter ○ Card & Newsletter	○ Family Portrait			
Name:	Sent ○	Sent ○	Sent ○	Sent ○
Address:	Rec'd ○	Rec'd ○	Rec'd ○	Rec'd ○
	Notes:			
City, State, Zip:				
○ Card ○ Newsletter ○ Card & Newsletter	○ Family Portrait			
Name:	Sent ○	Sent ○	Sent ○	Sent ○
Address:	Rec'd ○	Rec'd ○	Rec'd ○	Rec'd ○
	Notes:			
City, State, Zip:				
○ Card ○ Newsletter ○ Card & Newsletter	○ Family Portrait			
Name:	Sent ○	Sent ○	Sent ○	Sent ○
Address:	Rec'd ○	Rec'd ○	Rec'd ○	Rec'd ○
	Notes:			
City, State, Zip:				
○ Card ○ Newsletter ○ Card & Newsletter	○ Family Portrait			
Name:	Sent ○	Sent ○	Sent ○	Sent ○
Address:	Rec'd ○	Rec'd ○	Rec'd ○	Rec'd ○
	Notes:			
City, State, Zip:				
○ Card ○ Newsletter ○ Card & Newsletter	○ Family Portrait			
Name:	Sent ○	Sent ○	Sent ○	Sent ○
Address:	Rec'd ○	Rec'd ○	Rec'd ○	Rec'd ○
	Notes:			
City, State, Zip:				
○ Card ○ Newsletter ○ Card & Newsletter	○ Family Portrait			

Gift Planner

BOUGHT/MADE
WRAPPED
GIVEN

NAME	GIFT	BUDGET	✓	✓	✓
			☐	☐	☐
			☐	☐	☐
			☐	☐	☐
			☐	☐	☐
			☐	☐	☐
			☐	☐	☐
			☐	☐	☐
			☐	☐	☐
			☐	☐	☐
			☐	☐	☐

TOTAL ☐

Christmas Card List

Name:	Sent ○	Sent ○	Sent ○	Sent ○
Address:	Rec'd ○	Rec'd ○	Rec'd ○	Rec'd ○
	Notes:			
City, State, Zip:				
○ Card ○ Newsletter ○ Card & Newsletter	○ Family Portrait			

Name:	Sent ○	Sent ○	Sent ○	Sent ○
Address:	Rec'd ○	Rec'd ○	Rec'd ○	Rec'd ○
	Notes:			
City, State, Zip:				
○ Card ○ Newsletter ○ Card & Newsletter	○ Family Portrait			

Name:	Sent ○	Sent ○	Sent ○	Sent ○
Address:	Rec'd ○	Rec'd ○	Rec'd ○	Rec'd ○
	Notes:			
City, State, Zip:				
○ Card ○ Newsletter ○ Card & Newsletter	○ Family Portrait			

Name:	Sent ○	Sent ○	Sent ○	Sent ○
Address:	Rec'd ○	Rec'd ○	Rec'd ○	Rec'd ○
	Notes:			
City, State, Zip:				
○ Card ○ Newsletter ○ Card & Newsletter	○ Family Portrait			

Name:	Sent ○	Sent ○	Sent ○	Sent ○
Address:	Rec'd ○	Rec'd ○	Rec'd ○	Rec'd ○
	Notes:			
City, State, Zip:				
○ Card ○ Newsletter ○ Card & Newsletter	○ Family Portrait			

Name:	Sent ○	Sent ○	Sent ○	Sent ○
Address:	Rec'd ○	Rec'd ○	Rec'd ○	Rec'd ○
	Notes:			
City, State, Zip:				
○ Card ○ Newsletter ○ Card & Newsletter	○ Family Portrait			

Gift Planner

BOUGHT/MADE
WRAPPED
GIVEN

NAME	GIFT	BUDGET	✓	✓	✓

TOTAL

Christmas Card List

Name:	Sent O	Sent O	Sent O	Sent O
Address:	Rec'd O	Rec'd O	Rec'd O	Rec'd O
	Notes:			
City, State, Zip:				
O Card O Newsletter O Card & Newsletter	O Family Portrait			

Name:	Sent O	Sent O	Sent O	Sent O
Address:	Rec'd O	Rec'd O	Rec'd O	Rec'd O
	Notes:			
City, State, Zip:				
O Card O Newsletter O Card & Newsletter	O Family Portrait			

Name:	Sent O	Sent O	Sent O	Sent O
Address:	Rec'd O	Rec'd O	Rec'd O	Rec'd O
	Notes:			
City, State, Zip:				
O Card O Newsletter O Card & Newsletter	O Family Portrait			

Name:	Sent O	Sent O	Sent O	Sent O
Address:	Rec'd O	Rec'd O	Rec'd O	Rec'd O
	Notes:			
City, State, Zip:				
O Card O Newsletter O Card & Newsletter	O Family Portrait			

Name:	Sent O	Sent O	Sent O	Sent O
Address:	Rec'd O	Rec'd O	Rec'd O	Rec'd O
	Notes:			
City, State, Zip:				
O Card O Newsletter O Card & Newsletter	O Family Portrait			

Name:	Sent O	Sent O	Sent O	Sent O
Address:	Rec'd O	Rec'd O	Rec'd O	Rec'd O
	Notes:			
City, State, Zip:				
O Card O Newsletter O Card & Newsletter	O Family Portrait			

BOUGHT/MADE
WRAPPED
GIVEN

NAME	GIFT	BUDGET	✓	✓	✓
			☐	☐	☐
			☐	☐	☐
			☐	☐	☐
			☐	☐	☐
			☐	☐	☐
			☐	☐	☐
			☐	☐	☐
			☐	☐	☐
			☐	☐	☐
			☐	☐	☐
			☐	☐	☐

TOTAL

NOTES

Christmas
To Do:

NOTES

Christmas
To Do:

NOTES

Christmas
To Do:

NOTES

Christmas
To Do:

NOTES

Christmas
To Do:

NOTES

Christmas
To Do:

NOTES

Christmas
To Do:

NOTES

Christmas
To Do:

NOTES

Christmas
To Do:

NOTES

Christmas
To Do:

NOTES

Christmas
To Do:

NOTES

Christmas
To Do:

NOTES

Christmas
To Do:

NOTES

Christmas
To Do:

NOTES

Christmas
To Do:

NOTES

NOTES

Christmas
To Do:

NOTES

Christmas
To Do:

NOTES

Christmas
To Do:

NOTES

NOTES

Christmas
To Do:

NOTES

Christmas
To Do:

NOTES

Christmas
To Do:

NOTES

Christmas
To Do:

NOTES

Christmas
To Do:

NOTES

Christmas
To Do:

NOTES

NOTES

Christmas
To Do:

NOTES

Christmas
To Do:

NOTES

Christmas
To Do:

NOTES

Christmas To Do:

NOTES

Christmas
To Do:

NOTES

Christmas
To Do:

NOTES

Christmas
To Do:

NOTES

Christmas
To Do:

NOTES

NOTES

Christmas
To Do:

NOTES

Christmas
To Do:

NOTES

many thanks

Made in the USA
Monee, IL
12 December 2022